# EP Language Arts 5
# Workbook

This book belongs to:

_____

# EP Language Arts 5 Workbook

ISBN-13: 978-1986621939
ISBN-10: 1986621936

First Edition: April 2018

# About this Workbook

This is an offline workbook for Easy Peasy All-in-One Homeschool's Language Arts 5 course. We've modified and expanded upon the online activities and printable worksheets available at the Easy Peasy All-in-One Homeschool website (www.allinonehomeschool.com) so that your child can work offline if desired. Whether you use the online or offline versions, or a combination of both, your child will enjoy these supplements to the Easy Peasy Language Arts course.

# How to use this Workbook

This workbook is designed to be used in conjunction with Easy Peasy's Language Arts 5 Lesson Guide. As you and your child proceed through the Lesson Guide, use this workbook to exercise your child's language arts skills.

This workbook follows the EP online Language Arts course in sequential order, providing activity worksheets which can replace online activities and printable worksheets. However, this workbook does not include activity worksheets for the longer writing assignments. As such, this book does not contain 180 days of worksheets. The Lesson Guide will contain all writing assignments to make the course complete. There is also a brief description of them on the completion chart pages that follow (grayed out boxes denote no worksheet). If possible, allow your child to do these writing assignments on the computer to get practice typing and formatting papers.

The activity worksheets are designed with the following guidelines in mind:

- ## To supplement daily lessons
  This workbook on its own supplements, but does not replace, EP's daily lessons. Be sure to check the daily lesson on the website or in the Lesson Guide before having your child do the workbook activities.

- ## To serve as an alternative to online activities
  This workbook serves as an alternative to the activities posted online, providing offline activities in sufficient quantities and varieties to challenge your child. When used in conjunction with the Lesson Guide, this workbook becomes a complete offline course.

Please note, in the various places where nouns, verbs, adjectives, and adverbs are practiced, certain words can be categorized in more than one place (you can go for a swim [noun] or you can swim [verb]). If your child marks one of them differently than the answer key indicates, have a conversation with them to find out why.

- The solutions are on the website as well as in the Lesson Guide and are **not included** in this workbook.

# Completion Chart for Lessons 1 - 45

| | | | | | |
|---|---|---|---|---|---|
| (1) | writing - poetry | (16) | writing - poetry | (31) | metaphors/commas |
| (2) | spelling | (17) | sentence quiz | (32) | adjectives |
| (3) | writing - mood poem | (18) | noun quiz | (33) | misused words |
| (4) | writing - joyful stanza | (19) | grammar quiz, metaphors, spelling | (34) | grammar quiz |
| (5) | writing - funny poem | (20) | metaphors, similes | (35) | writing - short story |
| (6) | spelling/parts of speech | (21) | writing - diamante and sensory poems | (36) | writing - essay |
| (7) | adverbs/adjectives | (22) | writing - couplet, triplet, quantrain | (37) | writing/plurals/abbreviations |
| (8) | writing - season poem | (23) | writing - limericks | (38) | writing/capitaliation/punctuation |
| (9) | writing/parts of speech | (24) | writing - haikus | (39) | writing/pronouns |
| (10) | writing - psalm | (25) | writing - explorer poems | (40) | similes |
| (11) | writing - similes | (26) | writing - ten poems in a book | (41) | spelling |
| (12) | writing - similes | (27) | writing - review | (42) | writing/subject and object pronouns |
| (13) | writing - tangible/intangible | (28) | writing - anthropomorphic | (43) | writing/pronouns |
| (14) | verbs, imperatives, adverbs | (29) | spelling/punctuation | (44) | writing/irregular verbs |
| (15) | writing - intangible/unfettered | (30) | writing - short story | (45) | editing |

*Grayed out boxes denote writing assignments that don't have a corresponding worksheet in this book. Full writing assignments can be found online or in the Lesson Guide*

# Completion Chart for Lessons 46 - 90

| | | | | | |
|---|---|---|---|---|---|
| (46) | alphabetical order/ sentences | (61) | spelling/writing | (76) | writing - book review |
| (47) | writing - dialogue tags | (62) | spelling/writing | (77) | writing - book review |
| (48) | dialogue punctuation/writing | (63) | writing - sample story | (78) | writing - short story |
| (49) | dialogue punctuation/writing | (64) | complete sentences | (79) | comparative/ superlative |
| (50) | writing - fable | (65) | possessive nouns | (80) | word builder/verbs |
| (51) | parts of a story | (66) | spelling/ possessives | (81) | homophones/ spelling |
| (52) | subject/predicate | (67) | spelling/writing | (82) | writing - homophones |
| (53) | spelling/writing | (68) | adverbs | (83) | writing - response |
| (54) | spelling/writing | (69) | comma rules | (84) | possessives |
| (55) | writing - sample story | (70) | writing - letter | (85) | writing - response |
| (56) | spelling/writing | (71) | spelling | (86) | spelling/ conjunctions |
| (57) | spelling/writing | (72) | subject/object pronouns | (87) | writing - compare and contrast |
| (58) | compound, complex sentences | (73) | writing - book review | (88) | writing - compare and contrast |
| (59) | writing voice | (74) | descriptive words/book review | (89) | writing - compare and contrast |
| (60) | sentence structure/ word choice | (75) | writing - book review | (90) | writing - compare and contrast |

# Completion Chart for Lessons 91-135

| | | | | | |
|---|---|---|---|---|---|
| (91) | writing - compare and contrast | (106) | spelling | (121) | plurals/possessives |
| (92) | writing - compare and contrast | (107) | prepositions | (122) | grammar |
| (93) | writing - compare and contrast | (108) | writing/prepositions | (123) | writing - feedback |
| (94) | capitals/writing | (109) | writing/subject/predicate | (124) | prepositions/parts of speech |
| (95) | editing | (110) | writing - description | (125) | writing - friendly letter |
| (96) | capitals/irregular plurals | (111) | writing - improving weakness | (126) | spelling |
| (97) | plurals/commas | (112) | prepositions | (127) | spelling |
| (98) | past tense | (113) | prepositions | (128) | grammar/parts of speech |
| (99) | past tense | (114) | writing - nursery rhyme | (129) | summarizing |
| (100) | apostrophes | (115) | they're, their, there/spelling | (130) | spelling |
| (101) | writing/spelling | (116) | prepositional phrases | (131) | writing - short story |
| (102) | punctuation | (117) | prepositional phrases | (132) | writing - voice |
| (103) | writing/grammar | (118) | prepositional phrases | (133) | writing - irony |
| (104) | grammar | (119) | adverbs/prepositions/point of view | (134) | writing - organization |
| (105) | writing - paragraph | (120) | writing - fairy tale | (135) | writing - word choice |

# Completion Chart for Lessons 136-180

| # | | # | | # | |
|---|---|---|---|---|---|
| 136 | writing - main character | 151 | writing - setting | 166 | writing - novel |
| 137 | writing - plot/ idioms | 152 | writing - setting | 167 | writing - novel |
| 138 | writing - short story | 153 | writing - book outline | 168 | writing - novel |
| 139 | writing - short story | 154 | writing - book outline | 169 | writing - novel |
| 140 | writing - short story | 155 | writing - plot chart | 170 | writing - novel |
| 141 | grammar review | 156 | writing - chapter list | 171 | writing - novel |
| 142 | writing - book | 157 | writing - novel | 172 | writing - novel |
| 143 | writing/specific nouns | 158 | writing - novel | 173 | writing - novel |
| 144 | writing/protagonist | 159 | writing - novel | 174 | writing - novel |
| 145 | writing/adjectives | 160 | writing - novel | 175 | writing - novel |
| 146 | writing - sidekick | 161 | writing - novel | 176 | writing - novel |
| 147 | writing - antagonist | 162 | writing - novel | 177 | writing - novel |
| 148 | writing - sidekick | 163 | writing - novel | 178 | writing - novel |
| 149 | writing - conflict | 164 | writing - novel | 179 | writing - novel |
| 150 | writing/specific verbs | 165 | writing - novel | 180 | writing - novel |

Write a stanza of a poem in the same rhyme scheme as this stanza from *The Children's Hour* by Longfellow. (NOTE: the teaching lesson for this and every worksheet is located in the Lesson Guide. That separate book is necessary to make the course complete.)

*I have you fast in my fortress,*
*And will not let you depart,*
*But put you down into the dungeon*
*In the round-tower of my heart.*

_____

_____

_____

_____

_____

_____

_____

**Did you know?** Henry Wadsworth Longfellow had his first poem published at age 13. Don't let anyone tell you you're too young to do something great!

How are your spelling skills? Use a vowel pair from the box to complete the words below. Vowel pairs can be used multiple times, and some words can take more than one vowel pair.

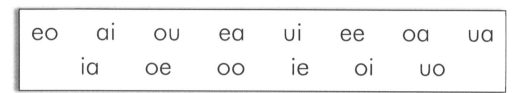

| eo | ai | ou | ea | ui | ee | oa | ua |
|----|----|----|----|----|----|----|----|
| ia | oe | oo | ie | oi | uo | | |

p___ple          g___de          ch___se

l___ve           c___t           h___ven

q___lt           g___rd          l___ves

q___te           n___se          th___gh

th___f           c___ked         y___th

fr___nd          ch___r          b___uty

can___           p___no          d___gh

# Lesson 3: Poetry Writing

Choose a mood to write about. Make a list of words that describe the mood or are synonyms of it.

_____

_____


_____

Write a poem in ABABCC format. Use at least three words from your mood word list. Here's an example.

> *Coming in through the door,*
> *"Long time, no see!" they offer big hugs.*
> *Suitcases laid down on the floor,*
> *They take a seat for fun on the rugs.*
> *All tickles and smiles,*
> *Happy they came the miles.*


_____


_____


_____


_____


_____


_____


_____

Write a joyful stanza with the same rhyme scheme as the stanza below from *Children* by Longfellow:

> *Ye open the eastern windows,*
> *That look towards the sun,*
> *Where thoughts are singing swallows*
> *And the brooks of morning run.*

_____

_____

_____

_____

_____

_____

_____

## Inspirational Quote
If you would hit the mark, you must aim a little above it: Every arrow that flies feels the attraction of earth.

-Henry Wadsworth Longfellow

Choose a poem from below and write your own poem with the same rhyme scheme.

I taught my dog the standard tricks
Like sit and stay and run.
But if my dog could learn to fly
We'd really have some fun!

I hope it doesn't rain today:
I have to go outside and play!
My attitude is not so fun
If I don't get a little sun.

Falling quickly from the sky
Catching rays from the shining sun
Clinging to lashes on my eye
Floating down until they're done
Snowflakes are a beautiful sight
Making the world look new and bright

_____

_____

_____

_____

_____

_____

Pick the vowel pair that fills in the blank to correctly spell a word.

b___t

oe    ea    ui    ua

l___d

ee    ou    uo    oo

tr___l

oi    oe    ai    eo

p___l

ia    ie    uo    ee

d___l

oo    oe    ua    ee

r___d

ou    oe    ui    oa

**Did you know?** Some nouns can only be plural. *Jeans*, *scissors*, *heebie-jeebies*, *tweezers*, and *underpants* are a few examples of **plurale tantum** (Latin for "plural only") nouns.

Circle the part of speech that correctly labels the underlined word in each sentence.

Is <u>anybody</u> home?           noun    adverb    pronoun

The <u>scientist</u> used a microscope.    verb    noun    adjective

This dinner <u>looks</u> good.        pronoun    verb    adverb

Power is out to the <u>whole</u> block.    noun    verb    adjective

We will be there <u>soon</u>.           adverb    noun    verb

Choose the word that correctly finishes the sentence. Is the sentence missing an adverb, or an adjective?

My son was acting _____ last night.
suspicious       suspiciously

He seemed _____ but would not tell me why.
excited       excitedly

I _____ asked him about it again this morning.
curious       curiously

He simply smiled _____.
happy       happily

He _____ ran to his room.
eager       eagerly

In a few minutes he returned, trying to keep a _____ look on his face.
serious       seriously

He _____ pulled a wrapped gift from behind his back and yelled, "Happy birthday!"
quick       quickly

I love my _____ little guy.
generous       generously

Choose a season and describe it in at least one stanza using the same rhyme scheme as the poem below (*Day* by Whittier).

*Talk not of sad November, when a day*
*Of warm, glad sunshine fills the sky of noon,*
*And a wind, borrowed from some morn of June,*
*Stirs the brown grasses and the leafless spray.*

_____

_____

_____

_____

_____

_____

_____

**Think About It**  For all sad words of tongue or pen,
The saddest are these: "It might have been!"
                                        -John Greenleaf Whittier

Underline the word in each sentence that is an adverb.

We are going to arrive soon.

He can jump high!

They quietly entered the silent library.

The giant panda was walking backward.

We always drink water with our meals.

The goofy dog leaped enthusiastically.

The Christmas story is very beautiful.

Circle the part of speech that correctly labels the underlined word in each sentence.

Singing is <u>somewhat</u> enjoyable.     noun     adverb     pronoun

My <u>daughter</u> plays soccer.     verb     noun     adjective

The band <u>was</u> exceptional.     verb     pronoun     adverb

My <u>favorite</u> sweater has a hole.     noun     verb     adjective

Express <u>yourself</u> politely.     adverb     pronoun     verb

Write a psalm that starts each line or most lines with "Praise Him!"

_____

_____

_____

_____

_____

_____

_____

_____

_____

**Doxology** Praise God, from whom all blessings flow!
Praise Him, all creatures here below!
Praise Him above, ye heavenly hosts!
Praise Father, Son, and Holy Ghost.                    -Thomas Ken

# Lesson 11: Similes

Write a simile for cold, soft, and hungry using *like*.

cold: _____

_____

_____

soft: _____

_____

_____

hungry: _____

_____

_____

**Here's a memory tip:** *Simile* sounds like *similar*. A *simile* compares two things that are *similar* using like or as.

Write three more similes. This time use *as* in all of them. As slow as… as funny as… as hard as…

as slow as _____

_____

_____

as funny as _____

_____

_____

as hard as _____

_____

_____

**Famous Simile:** A room without books is like a body without a soul. – Marcus Tullius Cicero

Write one **tangible** (physical, touchable) and one **intangible** (not tangible) thing that can answer these questions. If you can't think of answers to these, but you can think up your own questions and answers, feel free to use your own questions.

## What are big?

tangible: _____

intangible: _____

## What are thieves?

tangible: _____

intangible: _____

## What's good medicine?

tangible: _____

intangible: _____

**Think About It:** If malice or envy were tangible and had a shape, it would be the shape of a boomerang.

-Charley Reese

Tell whether the underlined word is an action verb, an imperative verb, or an adverb.

"<u>Hurry</u>!" shouted my mother. _____

The dog licked the bowl <u>greedily</u>. _____

Are you <u>jumping</u> to conclusions? _____

It will start getting colder <u>soon</u>. _____

I think our rehearsal <u>went</u> well. _____

Write a poem using at least two similes. Can you make your poem rhyme?

_____

_____

_____

_____

_____

Write sentences using the words *intangible* and *unfettered*, or see if you can write them both into one sentence.

_____

_____

_____

_____

_____

_____

**Did You Know?** According to research done by Johnson O'Connor, spanning more than twenty years and covering a wide variety of variables, across all ages and many different walks of life, a person's vocabulary level is the single best predictor of how successful they will be in the workforce. He also found that vocabulary usually comes before the success, and not as a result of it. Keep studying those big words!

Write a stanza in the same rhyme scheme as this stanza from the poem *Sympathy* by Paul Laurence Dunbar.

> *I know why the caged bird sings, ah me,*
> *When his wing is bruised and his bosom sore,*
> *When he beats his bars and would be free;*
> *It is not a carol of joy or glee,*
> *But a prayer he sends from his heart's deep core,*
> *But a plea that upward to Heaven he flings—*
> *I know why the caged bird sings!*

_____

_____

_____

_____

_____

_____

_____

# Lesson 17: Sentence Quiz

Language Arts 5

Answer the following questions about sentences. Learn from any mistakes!

Which of the following is a complete sentence?
- a. The talented photographer.
- b. He spends a lot of time perfecting his work.
- c. Photographs of birds and nature.

What kind of sentence is this: Don't forget to empty the trash.
- a. interrogative
- b. declarative
- c. imperative
- d. exclamatory

Use this sentence for the next 3 questions: The giant bulldog chased me down the street.

What is the simple subject of the sentence?
- a. me
- b. chased
- c. the street
- d. bulldog

What is the simple predicate of the sentence?
- a. giant
- b. down
- c. chased
- d. down the street

Which choice has a line drawn between the complete subject and the complete predicate?
- a. The giant bulldog chased/me down the street.
- b. The giant bulldog chased me down/the street.
- c. The giant/bulldog chased me down the street.
- d. The giant bulldog/chased me down the street.

Which of the following is not a run-on sentence?
- a. We traveled all over the country, we did it last summer.
- b. We visited many places The Grand Canyon was my favorite.
- c. My brother liked Carlsbad Caverns, my sister liked Niagara Falls.
- d. I had a great time, but nothing beats sleeping in your own bed.

Complete the writing assignment from your Lesson Guide.

_____

_____

_____

_____

_____

# Lesson 18: Noun Quiz

Answer the following questions about nouns. Learn from any mistakes!

Which list contains all of the nouns in this sentence?
The dog captivated the crowd with his leaps and daring flips.
      a. dog, crowd, daring, flips
      b. dog, captivated, with, daring
      c. dog, crowd, leaps, flips

Which sentence has all common and proper nouns written correctly?
      a. Last week Dad went to Metro Zoo with my brother.
      b. They saw lots of Grizzly Bears, Panda Bears, and Polar Bears.
      c. My Brother's favorite was the Churro Cart.

Which nouns correctly fill in the blanks of the sentence?
We picked lots of _____ from the _____ in the _____ .
      a. berrys… bushs… valleys
      b. berries… bushes… vallies
      c. berries… bushes… valleys
      d. berrys… bushs… valleys

Which nouns correctly fill in the blanks of the sentence?
While catching _____, the man used two _____ of cheese and some _____ .
      a. mouses… slices… potatoes
      b. mice… slicies… potatos
      c. mouse… slicees… potatos
      d. mice… slices… potatoes

Which answer has the same meaning as the words in bold?
**The ball belonging to the girls** went over the fence.
      a. The girls' ball
      b. The girl's ball
      c. The girls ball

Which answer has the same meaning as the words in bold?
**The brother of James** is named Andrew.
      a. James' brother
      b. James's brother
      c. Jame's brother

Which sentence has a line between the complete subject and the complete predicate?

        a. My brother and I went/to the library yesterday.
        b. We each/checked out two books.

What is the simple predicate of this sentence?
My mother washed the purple dishes in the sink.

        a. washed
        b. in
        c. washed the purple dishes
        d. in the sink

What is the subject of this sentence?
Please wash your hands and come to the table.

        a. hands
        b. your hands
        c. table
        d. you

Which answer has the same meaning as the words in bold?
**The uniforms of the officers** were navy blue.

        a. The officer's uniforms
        b. The officers' uniforms

Complete the following metaphors by filling in the blank.

His mind is _____.    Laughter is _____.

Her room is _____.    The moon is _____.

Add an –ing to the following words by dropping an e or doubling a consonant to spell them correctly.

hop _____    hope _____

share _____    run _____

# Lesson 20: Metaphor or Simile • Writing

Is the given example a metaphor or a simile? Circle the correct answer.

| | | |
|---|---|---|
| She has a heart of gold. | metaphor | simile |
| Her hair shines like the sun. | metaphor | simile |
| The snow was a white blanket. | metaphor | simile |
| We were as snug as a bug in a rug. | metaphor | simile |
| My brother is a couch potato. | metaphor | simile |
| Her tears fell like raindrops. | metaphor | simile |
| He's as fast as a cheetah. | metaphor | simile |
| She is a pig at the dinner table. | metaphor | simile |
| They ran like a herd of elephants. | metaphor | simile |
| The storm roared like Godzilla. | metaphor | simile |

Bonus tricky one:
My heart was a racehorse as I rode the rollercoaster.     m     s

Write a short poem using one metaphor.

_____

_____

_____

Write a diamante poem by following the instructions in the Lesson Guide.

_____

_____

_____

_____

_____

_____

Write a sensory poem following the instructions in the Lesson Guide.

_____

_____

_____

_____

_____

_____

# Lesson 22: Rhyming

Write a couplet, two lines whose last words rhyme.

_____

_____

Write a triplet, three lines with a rhyming pattern of AAA or ABA.

_____

_____

_____

Write a quatrain, four lines with a rhyming pattern of AABB or ABAB.

_____

_____

_____

_____

**Helpful Hint:** Do you struggle with writing poetry that rhymes? Try coming up with a list of rhyming words *first*. Then see if you can work any into a poem.

# Lesson 23: Limericks

Write two limericks. Here's an example:

*There once was a man named McGoo*
*Who painted his face red and blue.*
*But when we asked, "Why?"*
*He said with a sigh,*
*"I guess that I just wanted to."*

_____

_____

_____

_____

_____

_____

_____

_____

Write two haikus. Here's an example:

*Fine little snowflakes*
*Fluttering down to earth fast*
*A sight to behold*

_____

_____

_____

_____

_____

_____

**Fun Fact:** Haiku originated in Japan in the 17th century. Because so few words are used, imagery is a big part of most haiku poems. Traditionally, poets described aspects of nature in their haiku poetry.

# Lesson 25: Explorer Poem

Write a poem with facts from either what you are learning in history or in science. Make sure it rhymes to make it easier to remember the facts you're writing about. Here's an example about the Civil War:

*Abraham Lincoln was president*
*Which many people did resent.*
*One nation divided into two*
*South against North, gray versus blue.*
*Lincoln wanted the states united*
*Yet four long years, they were divided*
*The war ended in 1865*
*But many divisions are still alive*
*We must learn to love our fellow man*
*And with God's help, I think we can.*

_____

_____

_____

_____

_____

_____

_____

Write examples of each of the following: simile, metaphor, anthropomorphism, declarative sentence, interrogative sentence, exclamatory sentence, imperative sentence.

_____

_____

_____

_____

_____

_____

_____

_____

_____

Write an anthropomorphic story. Look around the room you are sitting in. Choose an **inanimate** object, something that's not alive. Write a short story as that object. Use the word "I" like that object is the one thinking and speaking in the story.

_____

_____

_____

_____

_____

_____

_____

_____

**Fun fact:** While anthropomorphism has six syllables, the word *scraunched* is the longest English word with only one syllable. It's the past tense of the word *scraunch*, which is the sound tires make when driving over gravel.

# Lesson 29: Spelling • Punctuation

Fill in the missing letter for the words below. Some are easy, some are hard!

| | | |
|---|---|---|
| bel__eve | tom__rrow | bas__ball |
| para__hute | independ__nce | calend__r |
| s__uirrel | def__nitely | ans__er |
| sep__rate | cou__h | __nife |
| suppose__ly | camo__flage | sc__ool |

**Did you know?** The diacritic dot on top of the lowercase letters i and j is called a tittle.

Fill in the missing punctuation from the sentences below based on the hints given.

Fill in 2 semicolons:
Lincoln, Nebraska  Juneau, Alaska  and Helena, Montana are state capitals.

Fill in 2 commas:
"I'm not sure" I said "that this the best route to the grocery store."

Fill in 2 commas:
July 4 1776 was on a Thursday.

Fill in 1 semicolon and 2 commas:
I used to dislike tomatoes green beans and lettuce now I'm enjoying their flavor.

Fill in 3 missing punctuation marks:
"Whats your name" I asked the small blond boy in the corner

Write a short story.

_____

_____

_____

_____

_____

_____

_____

_____

_____

_____

# Lesson 31: Metaphors • Commas

Answer the following questions about metaphors by filling in the bubble next to your choice.

What do metaphors do?
- ○ compare two unlike things using like or as
- ○ compare two unlike things without using like or as

Is this a metaphor? Her heart was stone.
    ○ yes          ○ no

Is this a metaphor? I'm as happy as a clam.
    ○ yes          ○ no

Is this a metaphor? It's easy, like taking candy from a baby.
    ○ yes          ○ no

Is this a metaphor? The mall is a zoo.
    ○ yes          ○ no

Write in the commas where they belong in the following sentences.

Surprisingly our team made it to the championship game this year.

As the underdogs no one expected us to win.

Being a new team it took us a while to find our groove.

To get us to bond as a team our coach took us camping.

At the campground we did many team building exercises.

After a while we started winning games.

Completely unexpectedly we took home the championship trophy.

# Lesson 32: Adjective Quiz

Answer the following questions about adjectives. Learn from any mistakes!

Which word in this sentence is an adjective?
The veterinarian gave a shot to the sickly dog.

      a. veterinarian      b. gave      c. shot      d. sickly

Which bolded word is not an adjective?
      a. We went to see the **travelling** circus.
      b. My sister enjoyed the **goofy** clowns.
      c. My **little** brother liked the elephants.
      d. My favorite part was the acrobats and their **flying**.

Which of the choices is the correct form of the superlative for the sentence?
That was the _____ sunset I've ever seen.
      a. colorful
      b. colorfulest
      c. most colorful
      d. most colorfulest

Which choice correctly completes the sentence?
Your handwriting is _____ than mine.
      a. best
      b. more better
      c. gooder
      d. better

Which words correctly complete the sentence?
_____ ball over there is _____ interesting shade of blue.
      a. That… an
      b. This… an
      c. The… a
      d. Those… a

What is the correct way to write the proper adjective in the sentence?
The south african choir blessed us with their beautiful music.
      a. South african
      b. South African
      c. south African
      d. south african

# Lesson 33: Misused Words

The underlined words are incorrect. Write the correct word on the line.

*Change the verb to match the plural subject.*
The twelve birds <u>sings</u> a song.                    _____

*Change the subject pronoun to an object pronoun.*
The teacher called <u>we</u> out for talking.            _____

*Change the verb to match the singular subject.*
My dog <u>fetch</u> his ball when I throw it.            _____

*Change the object pronoun to a subject pronoun.*
<u>Us</u> thoroughly enjoyed the movie.                   _____

Now it's your turn to find the incorrect word. Underline the incorrect word and write the correct word on the line. Can you fix the last two without a hint?

*Find a plural verb that disagrees with a singular subject.*
My friend Sam ride his bike every day.                 _____

*Find an object pronoun that should be a subject pronoun.*
Cade and me went to the library together.              _____

*Correct the pronoun.*
I'm going to teach they how to bake cookies.           _____

*Fix the subject/verb disagreement.*
The three little kittens loses their mittens.          _____

We'll all goes down to the park after our snack. _____

My sister dress her baby doll each morning.            _____

# Lesson 34: Grammar Quiz

Answer the following questions about sentences. Learn from any mistakes!

What is the simple subject of this sentence?
The huge rainbow in the sky was a beautiful sight.
     a. rainbow
     b. sky
     c. sight

What is the simple predicate of this sentence?
The children giggled loudly as they played in the yard.
     a. children
     b. giggled
     c. played

Which words correctly complete this sentence?
I had _____ my arm on the monkey _____.
     a. broke... bar's
     b. broken... bar's
     c. broke... bars
     d. broken... bars

Which contraction correctly replaces the words in bold?
We **should have** known the traffic would be bad today.
     a. should've
     b. should'of
     c. shoulda
     d. should'av

Which bolded word is an action verb, not a linking verb?
     a. It **seemed** dark outside.
     b. I **looked** out the window to see why.
     c. It **was** a rainy day.
     d. Maybe tomorrow **will be** sunny.

Which word correctly completes this sentence?
Wet socks are the _____.
     a. baddest.
     b. most bad.
     c. worst.

# Lesson 35: Writing

Write a short story using at least one simile and one metaphor. Get a high five and/or hug if you use more.

_____

_____

_____

_____

_____

_____

_____

_____

Choose a topic for your five paragraph essay and write it on the line. Then write a fact about your topic in each petal of the flower.

Essay topic: _____

Which choice is the correct spelling of the plural of the word in parentheses?

(Volcano) are fascinating parts of nature.

Volcanoes            Volcanos            Volcanose

The (deer) were drinking from the meandering stream.

deers                    deer                    deeres

The (hero) saved the day for the trapped hikers.

heros                    herose                    heroes

The various choices of cake (mix) made her head spin.

mixes                    mixs                    mixies

The (bunch) of (cherry) were squished on the ground.

bunchs... cherrys        bunches... cherries        bunchs... cherries

---

**Did you know?** Some nouns can only be singular. *Information*, *wealth*, and *dust* are a few examples of **singulare tantum** (Latin for "singular only") nouns.

---

Write the three main points for your essay on the lines below.

1. _____

2. _____

3. _____

Use the clues to help you rewrite the sentences correctly.

Find 2 punctuation and 2 word usage mistakes in each of these sentences:

"You is come to my house today" said Brandon

_____

Thats mine mom over their by the water fountain

_____

Find 3 misspelled words and 2 punctuation mistakes in these sentences:

The churchs on Spring Streat have steaples but the ones on Oak dont.

_____


_____

The potatos tomatos and peachs were all fresh.

_____

The underlined words are incorrect. Can you figure out why and fix them?

My neighbor <u>think</u> we are being <u>to</u> <u>noisey?</u>

_____

<u>You're</u> book is the <u>most big</u> <u>Ive</u> ever <u>scene</u>.

_____

Which pronoun correctly fills in the blank for the sentence?

Jamie and _____ went to the mall yesterday.
    I        me        myself

It was _____ who spilled the milk.
    I        me        myself

Mom asked Alan and _____ to clean up.
    I        me        myself

_____ share a closet since we wear the same size.
    My sister and I        My sister and me        My sister and myself

Dad was unhappy with _____ drawing on the walls.
    I        me        my

_____ report was the most interesting.
    Naomi and yours        Naomi's and your        Naomi's and your's

_____ choosing where we eat will upset everyone.
    My        Me        Myself

Between you and _____, I prefer the pink shoes.
    I        me        myself

Our giggling gave away _____ hiding spot.
    Jenny's and my        Jenny and my's        me and Jenny's

_____ are happy to share a pizza.
    Jason and me        Jason and I        Jason and myself

# Lesson 40: Similes

Remember that a simile makes a comparison using like or as. Use your creativity to come up with similes using the prompts below. Can you come up with at least four words for each line?

As happy as _____

As bright as _____

Colorful like _____

Beautiful like _____

Write a simile about your mom.

My mom is as_____

as _____

Write a simile about your favorite color.

_____is like_____

_____

Write a simile about your favorite animal.

A _____is as _____

as_____

# Lesson 41: Spelling

One of the underlined words in each sentence is misspelled. Can you correct it?

We all <u>tromped</u> down the <u>stairs</u> to <u>brakfast</u>.

_____

A <u>seargent</u>, a <u>colonel</u>, and a <u>captain</u> were all in uniform.

_____

My <u>chameleon</u> used his <u>camoflage</u> to hide from me.

_____

The dirty <u>landrey</u> pile was <u>completely</u> <u>ginormous</u>.

_____

How many words can you make from the letters in the box below? Only use letters that are adjacent to each other (see the example).

| C | L | A | S | E | L | A | R |
|---|---|---|---|---|---|---|---|
| M | I | S | H | E | F | L | Y |
| E | S | H | T | A | N | K | S |
| L | P | E | O | L | C | N | P |
| O | A | T | U | S | T | E | A |
| N | E | O | E | L | T | K | S |
| C | S | E | S | E | D | L | T |
| H | R | H | T | C | A | H | M |
| A | I | C | A | R | N | T | A |

_____ claims _____          _____

_____          _____

_____          _____

_____          _____

# Lesson 42: Subject and Object Pronouns

Fill in the missing pronouns with one of the choices. Does the sentence need an object pronoun or a subject pronoun?

Ezra, Briley, and I went to the store. _____ bought cookies.
                 We         Us

Michael kicked the ball that fell right at _____ feet.
            his         him

Daniel and Nathaniel are friends. _____ do a lot together.
            Them       They

_____ are happy to help. We won't complain.
       We         Us

Is this invitation for _____ or for you?
           me        I

Brooke made herself a new skirt. It fit _____ perfectly.
           she        her

Peter, Samuel, and Andrew play chess and _____ are good.
           them       they

Chase and _____ are the chess champions.
           me        I

Braden and Bristol can juggle because I taught _____.
           them       they

You should learn badminton from Iris and _____.
           me        I

# Lesson 43: Pronouns

Circle the pronoun that best fits the blank.

Try to do it by _____ next time.          myself   yourself   you

Matthew earned _____ own money.          him      your      his

Jessica and Kaitlyn called _____ mom.    their    her       his

Can _____ please feed the cat?           you      us        her

Ashlyn sang a solo by _____.             yourself herself   her

The problem solved _____.                itself   him       me

Joshua is smart. _____ likes math.       Him      His       He

Karl and Jenn cleaned _____ home.        its      their     me

Alex wears glasses. _____ likes them.    Her      She       Hers

Eliana's dress is so bright _____ shines.  her    it        he

_____ will be late to the play.          We       Them      Her

John and _____ went to church.           my       me        I

_____ wanted to start a business.        Them     Her       He

Listen to Dad and _____.                 my       me        I

Which irregular past tense verb best fills in the blank in the sentence? Learn from any mistakes!

The storm _____ to let up after its utter deluge.
     a. begun     b. began     c. beginned

Liam _____ a lifelike rendition of Dr. Martin Luther King, Jr.
     a. drew     b. drawed     c. drawn

My dad is good with tools and _____ us a backyard treehouse.
     a. builded     b. build     c. built

A gentle breeze _____ on that fine, spring morning.
     a. blown     b. blew     c. blowed

We _____ the candles on the cake and promptly set off the smoke alarm.
     a. lighted     b. lited     c. lit

Isaac _____ the football so hard it left a mark on my hand.
     a. threw     b. throwed     c. through

The area rug was full of dust and dog hair so we _____ it outside.
     a. shaked     b. shaken     c. shook

We all _____ the shooting star as it streaked across the sky.
     a. saw     b. seen     c. had saw

I _____ the entire week trying to build my new Lego set.
     a. spended     b. spent     c. spend

Rebecca _____ her lunch to school every day.
     a. brung     b. brang     c. brought

Sara _____ the balloon the most during the balloon toss.
     a. catched     b. caught     c. cot

Our house _____ the third day on the market.
     a. selled     b. saled     c. sold

# Lesson 45: Editing Checklist

Read through your essay and fix any mistakes. Here is an editing checklist. Aim for a check mark in each box.

## Introduction

☐ My introduction begins with an attention grabber.
☐ My introduction has at least three sentences.
☐ My introduction ends with the main idea of my essay.

## Body

☐ The body of my essay has at least three paragraphs.
☐ Each paragraph of the body starts with a topic sentence.
☐ Each paragraph of the body has at least three supporting sentences.
☐ Each paragraph of the body has a conclusion sentence.

## Conclusion

☐ My conclusion has at least three sentences.
☐ My conclusion restates my main idea.
☐ My conclusion answers the question, "So what?"

## Unity

☐ My essay flows well and makes sense.
☐ My essay uses transition words.
☐ My essay is interesting.

## Subject Matter

☐ My essay has different sentences – short, long, compound, complex.
☐ My essay uses descriptive words.
☐ All parts of my essay support my main idea.

## Grammar/Mechanics

☐ All words are spelled correctly.
☐ There are no grammatical mistakes.
☐ There are no punctuation errors.
☐ There are no fragments.
☐ There are no run-on sentences.

# Lesson 46: Alphabetical Order • Sentences Language Arts 5

Put these lists in alphabetical order. If the first letters match, move on to the second letter, and on down the line until you find different letters.

January, February, March, April, May, June, July, August, September, October, November, December

_____

_____

strawberry, bridge, strap, bring, falcon, plentiful, fabulous, plantation, straw, football

_____

_____

Put a check mark if the sentence is complete. If it's not complete, make it a complete sentence using the lines provided.

All of the beautiful leaves of red, orange, and yellow.

_____

I am sad.

_____

The juicy burger satisfied my hunger.

_____

Christmas morning at the Rutherford household.

_____

Write a dialogue between two animals.

_____

_____

_____

_____

_____

_____

_____

_____

_____

_____

Do you remember how to properly punctuate dialogue? Fill in the bubble next to the sentence that is punctuated properly.

○  "I am ready to go home now." said Amanda.
○ "I am ready to go home now" said Amanda.
○ "I am ready to go home now," said Amanda.

○  "Well", I replied, "I'm not quite ready to go."
○ "Well," I replied, "I'm not quite ready to go."
○ "Well" I replied "I'm not quite ready to go".

○ "Is there anything I can do to help you?" Amanda asked.
○ "Is there anything I can do to help you"? Amanda asked.
○ "Is there anything I can do to help you," Amanda asked?

○ I answered, "Let me think."
○ I answered "Let me think."
○ I answered, "Let me think".

○ "Oh, I've got it," I exclaimed!
○ "Oh, I've got it!" I exclaimed.
○ "Oh, I've got it" I exclaimed.

○ "You can find my keys," I suggested, "we need those to leave."
○ "You can find my keys", I suggested. "We need those to leave".
○ "You can find my keys," I suggested. "We need those to leave."

○ "They're in your hand!" she laughed.
○ "They're in your hand," she laughed!
○ "They're in your hand." She laughed.

(continued on next page)

Write a dialogue between two characters in history. King Tut and Neil Armstrong;
Martin Luther King, Jr. and Genghis Khan… whomever you like!

_____

_____

_____

_____

_____

_____

_____

_____

_____

_____

"I walked on
the moon!"

Correct these sentences. Add all missing punctuation and underline words that should be capitalized.

i have two cats  peggy said  do you have any pets

i have two dogs  said joe  as well as three fish and seven snails

i work at a pet store  said jeremy  does that count

i'm not sure  said sue if ive ever had a pet

Write a dialogue between you and someone in your family OR anyone you like.

_____

_____

_____

_____

_____

_____

_____

Write a fable with the moral, "It's what's on the inside that counts."

_____

_____

_____

_____

_____

_____

_____

_____

_____

**Think About It:** What does the Bible have to say about this? Look up 1 Samuel 16:7 to see what God said when others saw a shepherd boy, but He saw a king. Then look up 1 Peter 3:3-4 to see what He considers to be unfading beauty that is of great worth.

Answer these questions about the different elements of a story.

Which of these would be the **setting** of a fairytale?

    a. a kingdom far, far away and long, long ago
    b. a prince or princess

Which of these describes the **characters** in a story?

    a. where the story takes place
    b. who is involved in the story, both heroes and villains

Which of these might be the **plot** of a story?

    a. Colonial America, 1600s
    b. Against all odds, a group of dreamers breaks away from the rule of their country to start a new life in a new world.

Which of these describes the **conflict** of a story?

    a. the problem the main character needs to solve
    b. when two characters in the story fight each other

What happens in the **climax** of the story?

    a. the conflict is resolved, often by a villain being defeated
    b. the setting is revealed

What is the **resolution** of the story?

    a. the characters make fresh goals as a result of the climax
    b. we find out what happens to the characters after the conflict is resolved

# Lesson 52: Subject and Predicate

Underline the complete subject and circle the complete predicate.

The hall closet houses the mop, broom, and vacuum.

The never-ending movie rolled on and on.

My mom and dad have been married twenty-five years.

The bright red sock left balls of fuzz on the carpet.

The three girls were very chatty.

The lamp's light burned brightly in the otherwise dark room.

Write in the blank whether the underlined portion of the sentence is the complete subject (CS), complete predicate (CP), simple subject (SS), or simple predicate (SP).

<u>The boy's many chores</u> awaited. _____

The television set <u>blared loudly</u>. _____

Three dogs <u>chased</u> the ball down the road. _____

The blustery <u>wind</u> blew the curtains to and fro. _____

Her sympathetic <u>look</u> warmed my heart. _____

<u>I</u> am so very hungry. _____

The toddlers' giggles <u>were heard for miles</u>. _____

Fill in the lists below using the words in the box.

| | | | | | |
|---|---|---|---|---|---|
| match | bread | laugh | tread | plump | botch |
| knot | guess | tough | sense | clan | clamp |
| love | fluff | bench | pinch | lick | plug |

Short a spelled a

_____

_____

_____

Short a spelled au

_____

Short e spelled e

_____

_____

Short e spelled ea

_____

_____

Short e spelled ue

_____

Short i spelled i

_____

Short o spelled o

_____

Short u spelled u

_____

_____

_____

Short u spelled ou

_____

Short u spelled o

_____

(continued on next page)

Write a paragraph that tells how you would come up with money. Think of two ways — one reasonable, one crazy.

_____

_____

_____

_____

_____

_____

_____

_____

**Did you know?** According to various studies, those who spend their money on experiences rather than possessions are happier than those who do the opposite.

Use the words in the box to fill in the blanks below.

| match | bread | laugh | tread | plump | botch |
| knot | guess | tough | sense | clan | clamp |
| love | fluff | bench | pinch | lick | plug |

Write synonyms for the words below from the words in the box.

hard _____     giggle _____     mess up _____

seat _____     thick _____     family group_____

Fill in the sentences with the word that best fits from the box.

We should replace our tires since they have no _____.

These socks don't _____!

I have a big _____ in my shoelaces.

Can you _____ how old I am?

Your answer made no _____.

Don't _____ the spoon and put it back!

You forgot to _____ the tub and now the water is gone.

My cat is just a big ball of _____.

In a _____ I can substitute oil for butter.

(continued on next page)

Write a short story (it can be just one paragraph) about a problem and how you solved it. Save your story so you can find it later!

_____

_____

_____

_____

_____

_____

_____

_____

_____

**Did you know?** James Buchanan, the 15th president of the United States, used to purchase slaves for the express purpose of giving them their freedom. Talk about solving a problem!

# Lesson 56: Spelling

Fill in the lists below using the words in the box.

| | | | | | |
|---|---|---|---|---|---|
| claim | play | crave | cloak | meet | leap |
| slow | seam | kind | hide | splice | boat |
| yolk | creed | blow | laid | pray | haste |

Long a spelled a-e

_____

_____

Long a spelled ai

_____

_____

Long a spelled ay

_____

_____

Long e spelled ee

_____

_____

Long e spelled ea

_____

_____

Long i spelled i

_____

Long i spelled i-e

_____

Long o spelled o

_____

Long o spelled oa

_____

_____

Long o spelled ow

_____

_____

# Lesson 57: Spelling

Use the words in the box to fill in the blanks below.

| | | | | | |
|---|---|---|---|---|---|
| claim | play | crave | cloak | meet | leap |
| slow | seam | kind | hide | splice | boat |
| yolk | creed | blow | laid | pray | haste |

Write synonyms for the words below.


nice _____   tunic _____   not fast _____

jump_____   ship _____   quickness _____

Write the word in the blank that best replaces the underlined words.


I <u>have a strong desire to eat</u> pizza.          _____

The <u>sewn edge</u> of my shirt sleeve is splitting. _____

The <u>middle of my egg</u> is still runny.          _____

I <u>talk to God</u> first thing each morning.       _____

We went to see the <u>theater production.</u>        _____

I <u>affirm</u> that he is my dad.                   _____

I <u>set down</u> the baby in his crib.              _____

<u>Put out of sight</u> that chocolate cake.         _____

Can we <u>come together</u> at the mall?             _____

# Lesson 58: Compound/Complex Sentences Language Arts 5

Write whether the sentence is compound or complex on the line beside the sentence.

Some days are easy, and some days are hard. _____

If you want to come over, I can serve dinner. _____

When the phone rang loudly, it made me jump. _____

My dad had the steak, but I had the fish. _____

Add a clause from the box to complete each sentence. Write the letter of your choice and then whether the resulting sentence is compound or complex.

| | |
|---|---|
| a. If your bike tires are flat | d. and I need to go to the post office |
| b. but she couldn't | e. when you come inside |
| c. Should we start eating | f. Before you sign |

I need to go to the bank, _____. _____

_____, or should we wait for everyone? _____

_____, pump them up with air. _____

_____, be sure to read the entire document. _____

She tried to enjoy the movie, _____. _____

Please wipe your feet on the mat _____. _____

Write one compound sentence and two complex sentences on the lines.

_____

_____

_____

_____

Different styles of writing will lend themselves to different writing voices. Match the example sentence to the type of writing it represents.

      a. compare/contrast      c. persuasive argument

      b. personal narrative      d. humorous description

I believe homeschooling should be legal worldwide.      _____

I was thrilled to hear we were arriving at the park.      _____

Snails are small, but ladybugs are much smaller.      _____

Her hair spilled willy-nilly over her shoulder like pasta.      _____

Match the underlined portion of the paragraph with the "voice problem" it represents.

      a. slang      b. too formal      c. too informal

1. Our vacation was <u>totally rad</u>. 2. We went to Laguna Beach, California (<u>as if you needed to know the exact location</u>). 3. I and my <u>basic unit of society</u> had a really nice time together.

      1. _____      2. _____      3. _____

Add descriptive words and phrases to the sentences below, but keep them all in the same voice – don't mix formal and informal choices, don't be silly in one and factual in another. When you are finished, read through the whole paragraph out loud and see if it sounds consistent throughout.

Yesterday was a great day. The weather was _____.   I

went outside and _____

as I _____.

I could hear the _____.

Indeed, it was a marvelous day.

# Lesson 60: Word Choice

Which word choice strategy do the underlined words represent?

 a. strong verb          c. vivid adjective

 b. sense image          d. exact noun

1. The <u>pine</u> was swaying in the breeze. 2. It <u>towered</u> above the other trees as it covered and uncovered the sun, 3. <u>making dancing shadows on the ground</u>. 4. Its <u>majestic</u> limbs gently swung to and fro.

 1. _____    2. _____    3. _____    4. _____

Which of the options given is the more vivid word choice?

The river (meandered/went) through the woods.          _____

The soccer team was (hungry/famished).          _____

Let's go to (a restaurant/Big Mama's Deli) for lunch. _____

The snake (moved/slithered) along the path.          _____

Replace the underlined word in each sentence with a more vivid word.

I had <u>fun</u> at the fair.          _____

My brother is a <u>funny</u> guy.          _____

The ride home was <u>long</u>.          _____

We went to <u>the store</u> for snacks.          _____

<u>She</u> is my best friend.          _____

I thought dinner was <u>good</u> last night.          _____

Write a complex sentence.

_____

_____

# Lesson 61: Spelling • Writing Rubric

Fill in the lists below using the words in the box.

| fuse | lunar | loot | pew | cruise | feud |
|------|-------|------|------|--------|------|
| loom | accuse | fruit | mood | view | hooks |
| tooth | cook | books | flume | refuse | lose |

## The u sound found in *booth* spelled:

oo

_____

_____

_____

u-e

_____

u

_____

o-e

_____

ui

_____

_____

## The u sound found in *few* spelled:

u-e

_____

_____

_____

ew

_____

eu

_____

## The oo sound in *crook*:

_____ _____ _____

(continued on next page)

# Lesson 61: Spelling • Writing Rubric

Use this writing rubric to assess your short story.

| | Advanced | Proficient | Basic | Below Basic |
|---|---|---|---|---|
| Ideas/ Content | ☐ Literary elements such as character, plot, setting, conflict, etc. are well-developed around a central idea | ☐ Literary elements such as character, plot, setting, conflict, etc. are somewhat developed around a central idea | ☐ Literary elements such as character, plot, setting, conflict, etc. are unclear or leave too many questions | ☐ Literary elements such as character, plot, setting, conflict, etc. are confusing or missing |
| Organi-zation | ☐ Paper has an effective, great introduction<br>☐ Conclusion provides resolution<br>☐ Structure is creative and clear | ☐ Paper has a good introduction<br>☐ Conclusion mostly provides resolution<br>☐ Structure is mostly creative and clear | ☐ Introduction is present but unclear<br>☐ Conclusion doesn't resolve the problem or tell us what happens next<br>☐ Structure is loose | ☐ Introduction is confusing or non-existent<br>☐ Conclusion is hasty or non-existent<br>☐ No obvious structure |
| Voice | ☐ Writer's voice adds interest<br>☐ Point of view is skillfully expressed | ☐ Writer's voice is fitting<br>☐ Point of view is evident | ☐ Writer's voice is repetitive<br>☐ Point of view is confusing | ☐ No sense of voice<br>☐ Point of view is missing |
| Word/ Language Choice | ☐ Words are used appropriately<br>☐ Figurative language included | ☐ Words are used well<br>☐ Descriptions are satisfactory | ☐ Words and meanings are vague<br>☐ Descriptions lacking | ☐ Limited vocabulary utilized<br>☐ Descriptive language absent |
| Sentence Fluency | ☐ Sentence structure enhances story<br>☐ Transitions used between sentences and paragraphs | ☐ Varied sentence structure evident<br>☐ Transitions present | ☐ Sentence structure repetitive<br>☐ Limited transitional phrases | ☐ Rambling or awkward sentences<br>☐ Transitions missing |

# Lesson 62: Spelling

Use the words in the box to fill in the blanks below.

| | | | | | |
|---|---|---|---|---|---|
| fuse | lunar | loot | pew | cruise | feud |
| loom | accuse | fruit | mood | view | hooks |
| tooth | cook | books | flume | refuse | lose |

Write synonyms for the words below.

molar _____     bake _____     fight _____

treasure_____     deny _____     sight_____

Fill in the sentences with the word that best fits.

I think we might have blown a _____.

Don't bother him; he's in a bad _____.

You should be a good sport, even when you _____.

Did you see the _____ eclipse?

Make sure you eat enough _____.

Did you _____ me of lying?

The coats were all hanging on the _____ in the closet.

We sat down on the hard _____.

That's a large stack of _____!

# Lesson 64: Complete Sentences

Write C if the words make a complete sentence. Write F is the words make a sentence fragment. Write RO if the words make a run-on sentence.

It's summer! _____

Time to go to the pool. _____

I love to float on my back in the water. _____

Sunscreen, towels, sunglasses, and dive sticks. _____

I like the sun I like the water. _____

Correct the run-on sentences by writing *and*, *but*, or *or* on the line and adding a comma where you would add them to make a compound sentence.

I want to play I am sick today. _____

Do you like pizza do you prefer hot dogs? _____

I like vacation there's no place like home. _____

My favorite color is blue I also like red. _____

We could watch a movie we could play a game. _____

Turn these sentence fragments into complete sentences on the lines.

Early on Saturday morning.

_____

The pile of dirty laundry.

_____

Running and jumping.

_____

The book on the table.

_____

On the first line, write whether the noun is singular (S) or plural (P). On the second line, make the noun possessive.

foxes    \_\_\_\_ _____     Riley    \_\_\_\_ _____

children    \_\_\_\_ _____     houses    \_\_\_\_ _____

book    \_\_\_\_ _____     men    \_\_\_\_ _____

money    \_\_\_\_ _____     deer    \_\_\_\_ _____

papers    \_\_\_\_ _____     cherries    \_\_\_\_ _____

Change the underlined words into possessive nouns by either writing in an apostrophe or an apostrophe s.

The <u>dolphins</u> tails were slapping the water.

We went to the <u>children</u> museum last week.

<u>Monday</u> power over <u>people</u> moods is pretty strong.

The <u>women</u> restroom had a long line.

The <u>Kellers</u> home was bustling with people.

We really enjoyed <u>Nashville</u> downtown scene.

The flood damaged all of the <u>books</u> spines.

Change the underlined words into possessive nouns.

<u>The theories of scientists</u> don't always agree.    _____

We played with <u>the cards belonging to Emily</u>.    _____

The <u>hula hoops used by the girls</u> were pink.    _____

Don't forget to bring <u>the sunscreen you own</u>.    _____

The <u>songs of the children</u> rang out beautifully.    _____

Fill in the lists below using the words in the box.

| | | | |
|---|---|---|---|
| march | stare | flair | chart |
| stair | heart | mare | bear |
| market | scarce | pardon | |

## The ar sound found in *far* spelled:

ar

_____                    _____

_____                    ear

_____                    _____

## The air sound found in *chair* spelled:

are                                        air

_____                    _____

_____                    _____

ar-e                                       ear

_____                    _____

Write a possessive noun into the blanks in the sentences.

My _____ computer is on the fritz.

The _____ giggles filled the air.

A bunch of _____ heads appeared in the water.

We had a great time at _____ birthday party.

Your _____ water bowl is empty.

Use the words in the box to fill in the blanks below.

| | | | |
|---|---|---|---|
| march | stare | flair | chart |
| stair | heart | mare | bear |
| market | scarce | pardon | |

Write synonyms for the words below.

step _____     horse _____     store _____

few _____     gaze _____     pizazz_____

Fill in the sentences with the word that best fits.

Exercise is good for your _____.

Show me the graph from your _____.

This burden is too much to _____.

Please _____ me, for I need to leave early.

The band likes to _____ in formation.

Write a short description of your favorite place in nature. See if you can use possessive nouns to make your writing better.

_____

_____

_____

_____

Each of these sentences has too many adverbs. Choose one adverb and cross the others out so the sentence is more readable.

Our big family frequently runs out of milk often.

They boisterously ran around the room loudly.

We occasionally usually go to the park normally.

The girls were overly, amazingly, extremely excited it was Christmas.

Please quickly come here immediately!

We will soon be going shortly.

She quietly whispered to her sister softly.

Write your own adverb in the blank, using the words in parentheses to guide you as to what type of adverb to use.

The class sat _____ as they waited for the teacher. (how)

I left my book _____ by the table. (where)

We _____ go to church on Sundays. (when)

Sheila recites multiplication facts _____. (how)

I _____ enjoy the symphony. (how)

I'm sure it's _____, we just need to look. (where)

_____, we will go to the zoo. (when)

# Lesson 69: Commas

Which of the choices have the commas in the right places? Fill in the bubble next to your answer.

○ We can play the game, but we need to clean our room first.
○ We can play the game but we need to clean our room, first.
○ We can play, the game, but we need to clean our room first.

○ Understandably she was upset at the news, that her dog had died.
○ Understandably, she was upset at the news that her dog had died.
○ Understandably, she was upset at the news, that her dog had died.

○ We are going to San Antonio Texas, after Thanksgiving.
○ We are going to San Antonio, Texas, after Thanksgiving.
○ We are going to San Antonio, Texas after Thanksgiving.

○ The purple, green, and blue flowers made a lovely bouquet.
○ The purple green and blue flowers, made a lovely bouquet.
○ The purple green and blue, flowers made a lovely bouquet.

○ After a long day at the park we were ready for some water.
○ After a long day at the park, we were ready for some water.
○ After a long day, at the park, we were ready for some water.

○ The twins were born on Friday, October 27, 2006.
○ The twins were born on Friday October 27, 2006.
○ The twins were born on Friday, October 27 2006.

○ We can't find the hammer, but, we can find the wrench.
○ We can't find the hammer, but we can find the wrench.
○ We can't find, the hammer, but we can find, the wrench.

○ If I don't, have your number how can I call you?
○ If, I don't have your number how can I call you?
○ If I don't have your number, how can I call you?

○ Dusty our 80 pound dog, still thinks he's a tiny puppy.
○ Dusty, our 80 pound dog, still thinks he's a tiny puppy.
○ Dusty, our 80 pound dog still thinks he's a tiny puppy.

Write a letter to a friend that tells the story of something you lost and how you found it. Using commas correctly, list all the places you looked and all the people who helped you find it.

_____

_____

_____

_____

_____

_____

_____

_____

_____

**Did you know?** A comma is not just a punctuation mark. It is also a type of butterfly! The butterfly got its name because of the comma-shaped mark on the bottom of its wing.

# Lesson 71: Spelling

Fill in the lists below using the words in the box.

| | | | | | |
|---|---|---|---|---|---|
| firm | smear | swerve | turf | blur | church |
| leery | learn | cheer | career | rear | germ |
| fear | squirrel | adverse | first | fern | gurgle |

## ur sound in *turkey* spelled:

ir

_____

_____

_____

ur

_____

_____

_____

er

_____

_____

_____

ear

_____

## ear sound in *dear* spelled

ear

_____

_____

_____

eer

_____

_____

_____

# Lesson 72: Pronouns

Choose the correct pronoun for the sentence from the options given.

I would rather go with you than with _____ and _____.
- ○ him and her
- ○ he and she

Each one of the cars had _____ windshield broken in the hailstorm.
- ○ their
- ○ its

_____ runners like to have a certain kind of shoe.
- ○ We
- ○ Us

Sometimes, motorists don't seem to care much about _____ runners.
- ○ we
- ○ us

_____ and _____ don't always see eye to eye.
- ○ She and I
- ○ Her and me

The football team went to _____ bus.
- ○ their
- ○ its

The water droplets left _____ mark on the shower curtain.
- ○ their
- ○ its

We were planning to split the work between Jamie and _____. In the end, I did it all _____.
- ○ myself... myself
- ○ me... myself

Replace the underlined words with a word from the box by rewriting the paragraph on the lines. Put the words from the box into the correct tense to fit the paragraph. When you're writing, try to use descriptive words such as the ones in the box to make your writing more exciting and descriptive.

| ecstatic | adored | exhausted | excite | terrify |
| --- | --- | --- | --- | --- |

I <u>love</u> babysitting. I know it <u>scares</u> some people, but not me. Spending time with young kids is <u>fun</u> for me. I do come home at the end of a babysitting experience <u>tired</u> from all of my work, but it's worth it. I'm <u>happy</u> to think that one day I might be a parent and get to spend a lot of time with kids.

_____

_____

_____

_____

_____

_____

_____

_____

You discover a bottle that says "Drink me." Write a short story about your discovery, what you do with it, and what happens next.

_____

_____

_____

_____

_____

_____

_____

_____

_____

_____

_____

# Lesson 79: Comparatives and Superlatives

Fill in the blank with the comparative or superlative form of the adjective in parentheses. Use the sentence for clues as to which one it's looking for.

It's _____ in my home at night than it is during the day.
(peaceful)

My absolute _____ subject is math.
(bad)

I'm _____ at science than history.
(good)

Her hit went the _____ of all.
(far)

The fire truck's siren is _____ than our car's horn.
(loud)

The _____ month of the year at my house is August.
(hot)

Your ice cream cone is _____ than mine.
(big)

The sky is _____ than it was last night.
(colorful)

This is the _____ rose I've ever seen!
(red)

My mom is _____ than my sister.
(short)

This is the _____ he's been in a long time.
(happy)

How many words can you make from the letters in the box below? Only use letters that are adjacent to each other (see the example).

| C | L | A | L | A | C | R | A |
|---|---|---|---|---|---|---|---|
| M | I | N | T | P | O | S | M |
| R | S | E | A | E | R | A | T |
| A | R | K | O | H | K | E | Y |
| I | A | N | H | S | L | R | O |
| N | D | O | S | I | E | L | H |
| S | T | K | I | W | D | N | G |
| H | R | H | S | E | I | U | N |
| O | I | P | U | L | L | E | T |

claims

_____          _____

_____          _____

_____          _____

_____          _____

Identify the verb type that is underlined.

We <u>can't</u> go to the movies.
main verb   helping verb   contraction

We <u>are</u> going to dinner.
main verb   helping verb   contraction

Next week we'll <u>try</u> a movie.
main verb   helping verb   contraction

I <u>have</u> a theater coupon.
main verb   helping verb   contraction

# Lesson 81: Homophones • Word Search

Choose the correct homophone to fill in the blank of the sentence.

_____ going home.
Their      They're      There

Is that _____ book?
your        you're

Go _____ the tunnel.
through        threw

My laces are in a _____.
not        knot

The trailer on the truck will _____ the _____ to the farm.
hall... hey      haul... hey      hall... hay      haul... hay

Find the words below in the word search. Words are hidden in all directions.

```
Q  K  B  O  O  I  J  U  A  B  S  P  N  N  N
U  G  D  O  W  N  L  O  A  D  T  O  Q  P  V
B  A  L  C  O  N  Y  N  H  U  I  N  R  L  R
J  K  S  F  S  B  O  E  U  T  R  E  C  T  W
J  F  W  A  K  U  S  V  A  L  T  I  Z  D  D
A  V  Q  V  R  K  P  Z  O  P  Y  G  W  E  B
C  W  A  R  S  T  I  P  C  G  Y  H  E  W  J
Y  C  K  N  A  L  I  E  O  K  T  B  B  Q  S
I  J  T  W  I  V  Y  S  C  S  J  O  S  Y  G
M  D  A  V  A  S  A  G  T  V  E  R  I  W  J
I  R  I  E  Y  R  H  G  B  I  L  D  T  O  G
W  C  R  Q  N  Q  D  K  E  I  C  F  E  T  R
```

| | |
|---|---|
| artistic | neighbor |
| awkward | ravage |
| balcony | supposed |
| civilization | vanish |
| download | website |

Write a short story using a pair of homophones.

_____

_____

_____

_____

_____

_____

_____

_____

_____

**Memory tip:** Homophones are words that _sound_ alike but have different spellings and meanings. Think of a _phone_ and that you use it to _hear_ what the other person is saying to you, and that can help you remember that homophones _sound_ alike.

Should people mind their own business or not? Which is better and why? Answer in complete sentences.

_____

_____

_____

_____

_____

_____

_____

_____

**Get the Juices Flowing:** Along the lines of this assignment, can you think of a time when you didn't mind your own business and it turned out differently than someone would expect? How about in history? Can you think of a time when someone intervened in someone else's business and good things came of it? Or how about a time when someone stayed out of it because it wasn't their business and it ended badly?

# Lesson 84: Possessive Nouns

Choose the correct sentence of each group of choices.

○ The game's design was superb.
○ The games' design was superb.
○ The games's design was superb.

○ The shows' credits ran on and on.
○ The show's credits ran on and on.
○ The showes credits ran on and on.

○ The childrens' game was over quickly.
○ The childrens's game was over quickly.
○ The children's game was over quickly.

○ Its always nice when it's sunny outside.
○ It's always nice when its sunny outside.
○ It's always nice when it's sunny outside.

○ The two city's streets intersected at the county line.
○ The two citie's streets intersected at the county line.
○ The two cities' streets intersected at the county line.

○ I've experienced three white Christmases.
○ I've experienced three white Christmas's.
○ I've experienced three white Christmas'.

○ Fridays' menu includes soup and sandwiches.
○ Fridays's menu includes soup and sandwiches.
○ Friday's menu includes soup and sandwiches.

○ Dr. Jennings' office called. Dr. Jennings is running late.
○ Dr. Jenning's office called. Dr. Jennings is running late.
○ Dr. Jennings's office called. Dr. Jennings is running late.

Write about what you think makes a good leader. Answer with complete sentences.

_____

_____

_____

_____

_____

_____

_____

_____

_____

Unscramble the following words taken from the book *Alice in Wonderland*. You can use the definitions given to help you figure out the word if you are stuck. The first two letters of each word are in parentheses after the definition for further help.

## CMOK

_____

not authentic or real, but without the intention to deceive (m, o)

## XACO

_____

to try to persuade someone (c, o)

## TDAIRCCNTO

_____

to make an opposite statement (c, o)

## OREVKOP

_____

to anger, enrage, exasperate (p, r)

## UEEVNRT

_____

a risky or daring journey or undertaking (v, e)

Choose the correct conjunction to connect the two parts of the sentence.

We can't go _____ you put your shoes on.
    so that        until        as if

Do your work now _____ you don't have to later.
    so that        until        as if

You look _____ you aren't feeling very well.
    so that        until        as if

# Lesson 87: Compare and Contrast

Use this page to help you brainstorm your compare and contrast writing assignment. You are comparing/contrasting the last two novels you've read. Today, fill out the way in which the two novels are similar. Here are some questions to help you brainstorm:

Who is the main character in each book?

What problem does the main character face?

Compare: ways the books are similar

Use this page to help you brainstorm your compare and contrast writing assignment. You are comparing/contrasting the last two novels you've read. Today, fill out the way in which the two novels are different. You might look at your list for how they are the same and ask yourself when they stop being the same.

Contrast: the way the books are different

Choose the sentence in each group that is capitalized correctly.

○ Mr. Mackey played the piano marvelously.
○ The giant pink Rabbit on the front of the card was creepy.
○ We had a Surprise Party for Ellie on Saturday.

○ The Atlantic ocean is smaller than the Pacific.
○ The Smartphone was so expensive.
○ We need to head east on Lake Street.

○ My dad's favorite show is *the Cosby Show*.
○ My mom prefers to read *Where the Red Fern Grows*.
○ My sister wrote a play called *West Of The Mississippi*.

○ Our favorite destination is rome, Italy.
○ George Washington was the first President of the United States.
○ I read an interesting article about Mickey Mantle.

○ "Let's go," Mom called, "for we're almost late."
○ "I'm not sure," Sally said, "What your point is."
○ William shouted, "come back with my ball!"

Answer whether each part of this letter uses proper punctuation.

Dear Sir or Madam:
    ○ yes          ○ no

Enclosed please find a refund for your endowment check to the metro zoo; our bee exhibit just didn't fly.
    ○ yes          ○ no

Sincerely,
John Hanson
    ○ yes          ○ no

# Lesson 95: Editing Checklist

Read your compare and contrast essay out loud. Change anything that doesn't sound right. Use this editing checklist to help you. Try to aim for a check mark in each box.

## Introduction

- [ ] My introduction begins with an attention grabber.
- [ ] My introduction has at least three sentences.
- [ ] My introduction ends with the main idea of my essay.

## Body

- [ ] The body of my essay has at least three paragraphs.
- [ ] Each paragraph of the body starts with a topic sentence.
- [ ] Each paragraph of the body has at least three supporting sentences.
- [ ] Each paragraph of the body has a conclusion sentence.

## Conclusion

- [ ] My conclusion has at least three sentences.
- [ ] My conclusion restates my main idea.
- [ ] My conclusion answers the question, "So what?"

## Unity

- [ ] My essay flows well and makes sense.
- [ ] My essay uses transition words.
- [ ] My essay is interesting.

## Subject Matter

- [ ] My essay has different sentences – short, long, compound, complex.
- [ ] My essay uses descriptive words.
- [ ] All parts of my essay support my main idea.

## Grammar/Mechanics

- [ ] All words are spelled correctly.
- [ ] There are no grammatical mistakes.
- [ ] There are no punctuation errors.
- [ ] There are no fragments.
- [ ] There are no run-on sentences.

Choose the sentence in each group that is capitalized correctly.

○ Let's go to South Carolina for our history trip.
○ The Psychology Test was really hard.
○ The Football team was on a hot streak.

○ We went to Paris on our last vacation.
○ Charlotte is in north Carolina.
○ My Insomnia is acting up tonight.

○ The seattle Space Needle is a tourist attraction.
○ We drove to Disneyland last Saturday.
○ His sport coat was a slick shade of Gray.

○ "Can you please come here?" my mother asked.
○ Is friday the last day of this month?
○ My favorite player is Ken Griffey jr.

○ My geography project was on south America.
○ The Strawberry Milkshake was so creamy.
○ We saw *The Tempest* on stage last year.


Make the words plural on the lines beside them.

mosquito _____     mouse _____

wolf _____     tray _____

goose _____     cactus _____

crisis _____     ox _____

Correctly write the plural of the word on the line.

person _____     tooth _____

calf _____     bush _____

radius _____     oasis _____

index _____     loaf _____

child _____     sheep _____

> **Did you know?** The correct plural of *octopus* is *octopuses*. *Octopi* became the assumed plural when Latin plurals were added to words, until scholars pointed out that *octopus* comes from the Greek. That makes *octopuses* the correct plural.

If a comma belongs in the box, fill it in. If no punctuation belongs in the box, leave it blank.

If you want good home cooking☐for a great price☐you should go to☐Mama's Little Bakery☐the best eatery in town.

Leaving for the wedding a little late☐we weren't sure if we would☐make it on time☐but we hit all the lights and got there☐right as the service was starting.

We were so excited for our aunt☐to come visit☐that we forgot to☐finish our school work☐for the day.

# Lesson 98: Irregular Past Tense

Choose the correct past tense verb to fit the sentence.

The wind _____ all of the leaves into the street.
    blowed        blown        blew

We _____ our dog to the vet.
    brought        bringed        brang

We have all _____ this movie already.
    saw        seen        seed

Your dog _____ my finger taking the ball.
    bited        bit        bitten

Mr. Hinkle _____ my dad's parking spot.
    took        taked        taken

We _____ the entire day at the park.
    spended        spending        spent

Pizza with pepperoni _____ my favorite meal.
    becomed        became        become

She _____ and skinned her knee.
    fell        falled        fallen

Choose the correct past tense verb to fit the sentence.

She _____ my hand tightly during the storm.

holded      held      hold

Mr. Gilman _____ the whole song by heart.

knowed      known      knew

Are you the one who _____ my bike?

stole      stealed      stolen

The president _____ at our local high school.

speaked      spoken      spoke

He has _____ a brilliant essay on slavery.

writed      wrote      written

The sun _____ over the hill.

rose      rised      risen

Her phone _____ so loudly it startled me.

ringed      rung      rang

We've _____ our bikes up that steep hillside.

ridden      rided      rode

Fill in the missing apostrophes from the sentences below. Remember that apostrophes show possession like *Mary's book* or *the three girls' dresses.*

Mr. Driscolls cat hopped up onto our fence.

Jamies car was a cherry red color.

The Randalls house was at the end of its street.

The four boys shoes were muddy from the rain.

Sams dog chased Tamaras rabbit across the street.

Patrices purses strap was caught in the cars door.

My two marbles went down the tracks hill.

The fireworks pops were loud to Tiffanys ears.

Will you grab Sues books and yours off the shelves?

The worksheets questions were full of tricks.

The bowls design made it perfect for chips.

Unscramble the following words taken from the book *Little Men*. You can use the definitions given to help you figure out the word if you are stuck. The first two letters of each word are in parentheses after the definition for further help.

## ESNIUTINA

_____

suggest or hint (something negative) in an indirect and unpleasant way (i, n)

## QITAUCA

_____

of or relating to water (a, q)

## OOPCCIEURS

_____

having developed certain abilities or proclivities at an earlier age than usual (p, r)

## ETMNUCEBR

_____

lying down (r, e)

## DNIETEMRT

_____

a cause of harm or damage (d, e)

## UVLACTTEI

_____

try to acquire or develop (a quality, sentiment, or skill) (c, u)

## MEAEGEINR

_____

a collection of wild animals kept in captivity for exhibition (m, e)

## ELAABIM

_____

having or displaying a friendly and pleasant manner (a, m)

Practice writing a long sentence.

_____

_____

_____

# Lesson 102: Proofreading

Correct the mistakes in the sentences below. Underline the words that need to be capitalized, cross out capital letters that should be lowercase or punctuation that shouldn't be there, and add in any missing punctuation. Some sentences have clues, but others you'll need to read carefully to make sure you don't miss anything!

Find 4 capitalization mistakes and 3 punctuation mistakes in each of these sentences:

my favorite authors are lewis tolkien and gunn

my friend, saras favorite movie is disneys *aladdin*.

youre a hard worker, My Mom said as i swept the floor.

Find 5 total mistakes in each of these sentences:

I like Winter and I like Summer too

my Aunt, does all of her shopping on amazon

cara was born on thursday march 4 2010.

You're on your own with these! Find the mistakes and correct them.

Dont touch the hot stove. Said dad

the Glue Stick was dried up when the girl's tried to use it

Last year chelles family went to utah to ski.

# Lesson 103: Proofreading • Writing

The underlined words are not correct. Write the correct word on the line.

The four girls <u>shares</u> a room. _____

The children read <u>its</u> books. _____

The teacher taught <u>he</u> class. _____

<u>Her</u> went to the library weekly. _____

Can I come to <u>you</u> house today? _____

Now you find the incorrect word in the sentence. Underline it and write the correct word on the line.

Not many people has seen that movie. _____

Many people is excited for Christmas. _____

Follow ours directions to the park. _____

She loves check the mail every day. _____

Would your like to ride bikes? _____

The cat ate all of their food. _____

Can you come with Sandra and I? _____

Write a sentence that is a list of things containing subjects and predicates.

_____

_____

_____

Fix the underlined part of each sentence by writing the correct sentence on the line.

<u>what</u> is your favorite <u>thyme</u> of year<u>.</u> <u>mine</u> is fall<u> </u>

_____

Mr. <u>doyle</u> played <u>Soccer</u> with the kids in <u>mexico?</u>

_____

I wrote a <u>Thank</u> <u>You</u> card to <u>nurse</u> Linda for her care.

_____

Now find the mistakes yourself. Write the correct sentences on the line.

doughnuts cakes and candies are nice in moderation?

_____

On are way to cedar point we had a flat tire.

_____

You're book was left, on the mantle, at grandmas.

_____

Write a paragraph about ways you are like or unlike a character from a book you've read.

_____

_____

_____

_____

_____

_____

_____

_____

**Why does it matter?** It can be easier to develop a character in your writing if you can base it on a real-life person. Figuring out how a character is like you and in what ways they differ from you helps you make them more interesting for your readers.

The underlined words are spelled incorrectly. Can you spell them correctly on the line?

The <u>dore</u> needs to be shut. It's cold <u>outsied</u>!

_____          _____

We <u>culd</u> go on the <u>rode</u> and ride our bikes.

_____          _____

The <u>blew</u> sweater is so warm and <u>fussy</u>.

_____          _____

Now find the mistakes yourself. Write any incorrectly spelled words on the line.

Tomorow is Independance Day in Amurica.

_____

The dog's tale was waging feuriously at the site of the cat.

_____

Can you poor me a dreenk? My glass is emptie.

_____

Remember that a preposition is always part of a prepositional phrase. Tell whether the underlined word is being used as a preposition or not by circling your answer.

The kids swam <u>across</u> the pool.          yes          no

The dog ran <u>through</u> the flower bed.     yes          no

Put the remote <u>down</u>!          yes          no

The bird soared <u>over</u> the trees.          yes          no

She loves to dress <u>up</u> her dolls.          yes          no

Quit horsing <u>around</u> and get to work!  yes          no

Underline the prepositional phrases in the sentences below.

Put the book on the table.

Come and warm up beside the fireplace.

You have what it takes within you!

Put the plant beside the window to give it more sunlight.

Read this story. It is full of prepositions. Can you underline each one?

My dog's name is Dusty. He's a busy dog. He loves to run around the coffee table. He likes to sit on the hearth of the fireplace. Sometimes he hides under the blankets of my bed.

He enjoys playing in the yard. When I accidentally throw his ball outside the fence, he tries to jump over the fence to retrieve it! Once he chose to do that rather than go through the open gate.

Dusty can be mischievous. He once buried my mom's gardening gloves beneath the maple tree in our yard. Yet he is the sweetest dog I know. When I'm scratching him under his ears and he's snuggled in my lap, all is right with the world.

Write a few sentences about an imaginative game that you have played.

_____

_____

_____

_____

In the following sentences, put a line under the subject and another over the predicate. Circle the prepositional phrase and draw an arrow pointing to the preposition. The first one is done for you.

Kinley and William gave their books to the librarian.

Would you like to have bacon with your eggs?

My father should be home around dinnertime.

Please grab the cereal from the pantry.

Iris put all of the DVDs on the shelf.

Chase piloted the plane above the clouds.

The boys played hockey until dark.

I love my brother's new bike.

Can you help me with the dishes?

Audrey hit the softball over the fence.

The girls ran all the way home from rehearsal.

Write a few sentences about a time that you apologized to someone for spoiling their fun and tried to make them happy again.

_____

_____

_____

_____

Write a story describing going somewhere and how you got there. Use at least ten prepositional phrases.

_____

_____

_____

_____

_____

_____

_____

_____

_____

_____

**Writing tip:** Are you looking to make your writing sound more interesting? Try putting a prepositional phrase at the _beginning_ of a sentence from time to time.

Write about a time when you wanted to "be good" or improve some weakness in your character.  Did you ask God to help you?

_____

_____

_____

_____

_____

_____

_____

_____

_____

**Did you know?** The Bible lists traits or "fruits" a Spirit-filled life will produce. Do you know what they are? You can look them up in Galatians 5:22-23. Is your life producing them?

Tell whether the underlined word is a preposition or the object of the preposition.

Andrew did his math worksheet <u>at</u> the table.
    preposition                  object of the preposition

Sandra and Jane rode their bikes to the <u>park</u>.
    preposition                  object of the preposition

Across the <u>river</u>, we found a neat trail.
    preposition                  object of the preposition

The cat was hiding <u>inside</u> the litter box.
    preposition                  object of the preposition

Can you fit everything in your <u>suitcase</u>?
    preposition                  object of the preposition

The object of the preposition is marked. Underline the preposition.

What time is it on the clock on the stove?

Beneath the surface of the earth, molten lava flows daily.

Hiking the snowy peaks of Mt. Everest is on my bucket list.

Have you heard the news about the Mexican earthquake?

There was a thunderstorm during the night.

Underline the preposition in the following sentences. Remember that a preposition has to be part of a prepositional phrase.

We enjoy swimming during the summer.

Don't try to walk across the busy street.

My dog chased a squirrel up a tree.

I would love to travel around the world.

I like playing dress up with my little brother.

We spun around on the merry-go-round.

Answer the following questions about prepositions.

Which of these words cannot be used as a preposition?
○ above      ○ between      ○ worse      ○ with

Which sentence has the preposition in bold?
○ I'd love to **go** with you to the concert.
○ My favorite group will be **singing**.
○ We can ride together **in** the same car.
○ We **can** sing songs all the way home.

Which sentence has the prepositional phrase in bold?
○ **I took my cousin** to the park.
○ He liked going up and down **on the see saw**.
○ He also enjoyed the slide because **it was really fast**.
○ It was hard to get him **to** come home.

Write a nursery rhyme. If you're having trouble coming up with an idea, make it about huckleberries.

_____

_____

_____

_____

_____

_____

_____

_____

**Did you know?** Huckleberry plants can take up to 15 years to fully mature (as opposed to, say, raspberries, which produce fruit the second year). Does it feel like you've been waiting for something for a long time? Some of the best things in life are worth waiting for. Hang in there!

Fill in each blank with the correct word. Each blank will either need *they're* (a contraction meaning *they are*), *their* (shows ownership), or *there* (a place).

We really enjoyed watching _____ soccer game.

What's that bright light over _____?

_____ mom said they need to come home.

_____ all tired from a long day at the lake.

_____ putting _____ books over _____.

See how many words you can come up with using the grid of letters below. Only use letters that are adjacent to one another as you have done in the past. This grid is smaller than the last one, can you still do it?

| E | R | A | T |
|---|---|---|---|
| F | M | L | S |
| O | E | R | U |
| D | I | C | E |

_____     _____     _____

_____     _____     _____

_____     _____     _____

Underline the prepositional phrases in the following sentences.

After the news, my favorite show comes on.

I keep all of my money in my piggy bank.

I went into the bedroom to get my book.

The eagle soared over the lake with elegance.

Let's go around the corner and see Grandma.

The woodpecker hit his beak against the tree.

I put my pulled tooth under my pillow.

Please get in the car so we can leave.

Big fireworks exploded above our heads.

The boat drifted on the open sea.

Our wheels spun rapidly as we flew down the road.

The rainy skies put a damper on our town parade.

The ponies trotted in a circle.

Could we go to the park today?

Using your same sentences from lesson 116, now underline the preposition and circle the object of the preposition. Remember that both of those will be contained within the prepositional phrase.

After the news, my favorite show comes on.

I keep all of my money in my piggy bank.

I went into the bedroom to get my book.

The eagle soared over the lake with elegance.

Let's go around the corner and see Grandma.

The woodpecker hit his beak against the tree.

I put my pulled tooth under my pillow.

Please get in the car so we can leave.

Big fireworks exploded above our heads.

The boat drifted on the open sea.

Our wheels spun rapidly as we flew down the road.

The rainy skies put a damper on our town parade.

The ponies trotted in a circle.

Could we go to the park today?

# Lesson 118: Prepositions

Fill in the correct pronoun to be the object of the preposition. If you're having trouble figuring it out, read the sentence out loud with both choices. Whichever one sounds right is probably the right answer.

Can you put a blanket over _____?       him      he

Let's go with _____ to the store.       them     they

Alyssa read a book to _____.            she      her

The bugs were swarming around _____.    we       us

Huge birds circled in the sky above _____. me      I

Behind _____ I saw a huge skunk.        him      he

Will you bring the phone to _____?        I        me

You can just go around _____.           they     them

She got what was coming to _____.       her      she

You are welcome to come with _____.     us       we

The blanket is under _____ so it's stuck.  he     him

She wants you to come to _____.         she      her

# Lesson 119: Adverb and Preposition Quiz

Answer the following questions about sentences. Learn from any mistakes!

What is the preposition and object of the preposition in this sentence?
The group of friends all had ice cream in little paper cups.

a. The/friends      c. had/ice cream
b. all/friends      d. in/cups

What is the complete prepositional phrase in this sentence?
The enormous rainbow could be seen over the rooftops all morning.

a. The enormous rainbow
b. could be seen
c. over the rooftops
d. all morning

Which bolded word is not used as a preposition?

a. Katie rode her bike **down** the street.
b. She turned to go **around** the corner.
c. As she turned, she fell **off** the bike.
d. That turned her smile upside **down**.

Which of the answers given is an adverb in this sentence?
My best friend goes to church here with me.

a. goes      c. here
b. to      d. with

Which choice uses the correct form of the adverb to fill in the blanks?
This cake is so _____; she bakes really _____.

a. good/well
b. good/good
c. well/good
d. well/well

Which words correctly fill in the blanks of this sentence?
We don't have _____ more crackers, and there _____ no peanut butter, either.

a. no/is
b. any/is
c. any/isn't
d. no/isn't

Choose a fairy tale you are familiar with. Rewrite the story from another character's point of view.

_____

_____

_____

_____

_____

_____

_____

_____

Choose the sentence of each group that is written correctly.

○ Those boys shouts are hurting my ears.
○ Those boy's shouts are hurting my ears.
○ Those boys' shouts are hurting my ears.

○ The other children's artwork is more colorful than mine.
○ The other childrens' artwork is more colorful than mine.
○ The other childrens artwork is more colorful than mine.

○ The horse had it's hooves cleaned by the stable boy.
○ The horse had its hooves cleaned by the stable boy.
○ The horse had its' hooves cleaned by the stable boy.

○ Why is the womens' room line always longer than the mens'?
○ Why is the womens room line always longer than the mens?
○ Why is the women's room line always longer than the men's?

○ All the area church's services were canceled by the hurricane.
○ All the area churches' services were canceled by the hurricane.
○ All the area churches services were canceled by the hurricane.

○ Drew's and Gracie's mom was PTA president.
○ Drew and Gracie's mom was PTA president.
○ Drew's and Gracie mom was PTA president.

Now you fill in the missing apostrophe(s) for the sentences below.

The peoples appointments were late when the doctor got a flat tire.

The cherrys stem was the ornaments hook.

Of the bolded words, circle the one that matches the part of speech to the side of the sentence.

We all **went** to the **busy restaurant** last **night**.   Adjective

I'm **too busy** to **do** it **myself**.   Pronoun

The **busily buzzing** bee **pollenated** the **flower**.   Adverb

I **want** to **go** for a **run later** tonight.   Noun

Can **you think** about **what** you want for **dinner**?   Verb

I listened **to** a **loud** storm **during** the **night**.   Preposition

**Yesterday** was the **Christmas parade** in **town**.   Adverb

**Today was** a **very** long **day**.   Verb

Have **you** been **to** the **bank** yet **today**?   Preposition

The **swirly** bubbles **floated through** the **air**.   Adjective

**His courage was obvious**.   Noun

**Will you** please **bring** me the **remote**?   Pronoun

Read this paragraph from the book *Little Men* and write feedback to the author on the lines below it.

The cat is a sweet animal. I love them very much. They are clean and pretty, and catch rats and mice, and let you pet them, and are fond of you if you are kind. They are very wise, and can find their way anywhere. Little cats are called kittens, and are dear things. I have two, named Huz and Buz, and their mother is Topaz, because she has yellow eyes. Uncle told me a pretty story about a man named Ma-ho-met. He had a nice cat, and when she was asleep on his sleeve, and he wanted to go away, he cut off the sleeve so as not to wake her up. I think he was a kind man. Some cats catch fish.

_____

_____

_____

_____

_____

_____

_____

Color in the bubble next to the list of prepositions in each group.

○ down, beside, behind          ○ tall, red, calm
○ fling, sprint, devour          ○ quickly, yesterday, soon

---

○ truly, madly, deeply          ○ up, to, with
○ run, jump, fly                ○ rosy, happy, fragrant

---

○ beautiful, fabulous, lazy      ○ always, only, usually
○ aboard, within, toward         ○ maple, novel, school

**Did you know?** There are 8 main parts of speech: nouns, pronouns, verbs, adjectives, adverbs, prepositions, conjunctions, and interjections. How many have you learned?

Write the part of speech of the bolded word in the blank.

I **only** have time for one more game.     _____

Would you like to **come** with me?          _____

Do you have the desire **within** you?       _____

That is such a **lovely** dress.             _____

The elegant **deer** leapt into the woods.   _____

Are you able to do it **yourself**?          _____

# Lesson 125: Writing – Friendly Letter

Write a friendly letter to someone.

_____

_____

_____

_____

_____

_____

_____

_____

_____

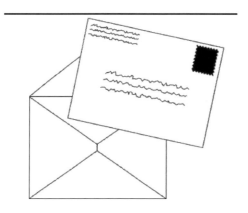

# Lesson 126: Loose or Lose

Choose the correct word to fill in the blank. By the end of the worksheet you should be certain which word has which meaning.

You'd better hurry up so you don't _____ your place in line.
    ○ loose            ○ lose

The whole dresser collapsed because of one _____ screw.
    ○ loose            ○ lose

Her _____ tooth made it hard to eat.
    ○ loose            ○ lose

Did you _____ any teeth yet this year?
    ○ loose            ○ lose

I counted all of my _____ change and can afford a drink.
    ○ loose            ○ lose

_____ the dog from the leash so he can run.
    ○ loose            ○ lose

The slower runner will _____ the 50-yard dash.
    ○ loose            ○ lose

I hope you never _____ your love of learning.
    ○ loose            ○ lose

The _____ board on the deck is a tripping hazard.
    ○ loose            ○ lose

Find the words from the book *Little Men* in the word search puzzle. Words can be any direction.

```
O P Y K T R X S R Y P E P R B J I
Z Y N E W P V G L Z L F B V D K G
Q Z C P X V F N Y B P Z H I E K S
I G G S V C H I A N E V G N V S X
B R I Q A J T C L M T K M G E E B
K I R H K L I O T E V W B R H T B
S A S E H L A V U A J I V A W V X
M L P Z P Y C B M Y R W U T U A E
T O M X J R A Y L T B V R I I G F
R B E N R P E R V E R S I T Y U V
V N F U L G U S T F V H O U C E W
I T V V X D F Q S X V H J D P L H
W H R W E C P H A I G X Y E T Y O
Z I N D I G N A N T B M J N B E T
V C Y P U J F V K W K L K K D E K
J M A G N A N I M O U S E C L H Y
C T H A X Q L C K K P T T G B F E
```

- indignant
- inexplicable
- ingratitude
- irrepressible
- magnanimous
- perversity
- salable
- vaguely

# Lesson 128: Grammar Review

Of the bolded words, circle the one that matches the part of speech to the side of the sentence.

The **kids went** canoeing on the **choppy lake**.    Adjective

Please **come** with **us** to our **delicious dinner**.    Pronoun

The **elephants loudly trumpeted** their **trunks**.    Adverb

The **blue** umbrella **shielded** us **from** the **rain**.    Noun

The **sweet** sisters **held hands** as **they** skipped.    Verb

**We** ran **down** the **lane** as we **sang** the song.    Preposition

Write the part of speech of the bolded word in the blank.

I **pinched** my finger in the sliding door. _____

My sister's **sickly** eyes were red.        _____

The **lightning** flashed brightly in the sky._____

A gigantic river flowed **to** the sea.        _____

The **painfully** aching tooth throbbed.        _____

The massive fan blew **our** hair all over._____

Read each short paragraph. Then choose the sentence that does the best job summarizing the paragraph. For the last one, write your own summary sentence.

Genevieve was having a great kindergarten year. She had learned the alphabet and how to read small words. She had learned to count as high as one hundred. She knew lots of colors and shapes.

    a.    Genevieve knew the alphabet.
    b.    Genevieve could count high.
    c.    Genevieve was learning a lot in kindergarten.
    d.    Genevieve liked school.

If you have trouble with responsibilities, a virtual pet may be for you. You still have to feed it and clean up after it, but there are no real-life consequences if you forget or get lazy with it. Learn some responsibility with a virtual pet!

    a.    Virtual pets save puppies.
    b.    It doesn't hurt a virtual pet if you forget about it.
    c.    A virtual pet is cleaner than a regular pet.
    d.    Virtual pets are a safe way to learn responsibility.

Justin inhaled the cold air through his nostrils and smiled. He was giddy as the snow crunched under his feet. In his mind, nothing was better than exploring fresh snow and then warming up with hot chocolate. Winter was great!

_____

_____

# Lesson 130: Whose or Who's

Choose the correct word to fill in the blank. By the end of the worksheet you should be certain which word has which meaning.

Do you know _____ sweater this is?
- ⃝ whose
- ⃝ who's

I'm the only one _____ home sick today.
- ⃝ whose
- ⃝ who's

_____ afraid of spiders?
- ⃝ Whose
- ⃝ Who's

Gretta is a girl _____ hair is as bright as the sun.
- ⃝ whose
- ⃝ who's

That boy is Tommy, _____ father is in the army.
- ⃝ whose
- ⃝ who's

André is a boy _____ tough to beat in soccer.
- ⃝ whose
- ⃝ who's

I wonder _____ coming to the Christmas party.
- ⃝ whose
- ⃝ who's

_____ sponsor is Adidas?
- ⃝ Whose
- ⃝ Who's

_____ being sponsored by Nike?
- ⃝ Whose
- ⃝ Who's

Describe the main character of a story you've recently read for school. If this character were to be bullied, how would he respond? If this character was in a spelling bee, would she win or run away with stage fright?

_____

_____

_____

_____

_____

_____

_____

_____

**Writing Tip:** When you write a story, you want to know your characters inside and out. No matter what turn the story takes, you need to know how your characters are going to react.

Read the selection from the Lesson Guide. Describe the character's "voice." What's the tone? What are some things you think this character would say? What are some things this character would never say?

_____

_____

_____

_____

_____

_____

_____

_____

_____

# Lesson 133: Writing – Irony

Write an example of an ironic situation, something that's the opposite of what you would expect.

_____

_____

_____

_____

_____

_____

_____

_____

_____

Draw your main character or write your word and definition.

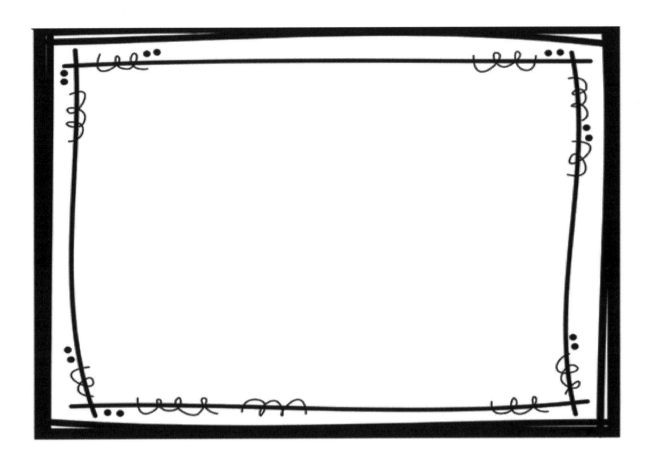

Make a list of at least three plot events. What's the character going to do first? Then what's going to happen? What are some things that the character could learn along the way? List a few ideas.

_____

_____

_____

_____

_____

_____

_____

Write the number of the idiom beside its meaning.

1. Bring home the bacon       _____   be really excited about something

2. Hit the nail on the head   _____   make someone mad

3. Deer in the headlights     _____   make money for your family

4. Drive someone up the wall _____   be in a bad situation

5. Have your ducks in a row   _____   be startled by something

6. Hit the hay                _____   be organized

7. Be on cloud nine           _____   go to bed

8. Be in a pickle             _____   get something exactly right

# Lesson 141: Proofreading

Answer the questions about the following paragraph. Use the numbers to help direct you to the right part of the paragraph.

1. Lightning is a fascinating phenomenon. 2. A single bolt of lightning is 54,000 degrees Fahrenheit. 3. A single bolt of lightning is about five times hotter than the surface of the sun. 4. Around the world, lightening strikes more than three million times a day. 5. That's about forty times per second. 6. It also kills around too thousand people a year. 7. Always respect the power of lightning!

Which of these is the best way to combine sentences 2 and 3?
- ○ A single bolt of lightning is 54,000 degrees Fahrenheit which makes a single bolt of lightning about five times hotter than the surface of the sun.
- ○ A single bolt of lightning is 54,000 degrees Fahrenheit and a single bolt of lightning is about five times hotter than the surface of the sun.
- ○ A single bolt of lightning is 54,000 degrees Fahrenheit, or about five times hotter than the surface of the sun.

What change should be made to sentence 4?
- ○ Remove the comma
- ○ Change *lightening* to *lightning*
- ○ No change

What change should be made to sentence 5?
- ○ Change *that's* to *thats*
- ○ Change *second* to *secont*
- ○ No change

What change should be made to sentence 6?
- ○ Change the period to a question mark
- ○ Change *too* to *two*
- ○ No change

# Lesson 143: Specific Nouns

Make a list of specific nouns that you could use instead of these more generic words.

tool          _____

tree          _____

things        _____

a drink       _____

furniture     _____

clothes       _____

flower        _____

dinner        _____

car           _____

food          _____

animal        _____

person        _____

a show        _____

# Lesson 144: Protagonist

Fill out this form for your protagonist. Some may not apply. You can draw a picture of your main character in the box.

Name _____ Age _____

Job _____ Hair _____

Clothes _____ Home _____

Family _____ Music _____

Hobbies _____

Sports _____ Food _____

Favorite things _____

Things (s)he can't stand _____

Does for fun _____

Bad habits _____

Fears _____

Quirks _____

Catchphrase _____

# Lesson 145: Adjectives

Write an adjective that starts with each letter of the alphabet. Use this page to help make your book more descriptive.

A _____

B _____

C _____

D _____

E _____

F _____

G _____

H _____

I _____

J _____

K _____

L _____

M _____

N _____

O _____

P _____

Q _____

R _____

S _____

T _____

U _____

V _____

W _____

X _____

Y _____

Z _____

# Lesson 146: Protagonist Sidekick

Fill out this form for your sidekick. Some may not apply. You can draw a picture of your sidekick in the box.

Name _____ Age _____

Job _____ Hair _____

Clothes _____ Home _____

Family _____ Music _____

Hobbies _____

Sports _____ Food _____

Favorite things _____

Things (s)he can't stand _____

Does for fun _____

Bad habits _____

Fears _____

Quirks _____

Catchphrase _____

# Lesson 147: Antagonist

Fill out this form for your antagonist. Some may not apply. You can draw a picture of your villain in the box.

Name _____ Age _____

Job _____ Hair _____

Clothes _____ Home _____

Family _____ Music _____

Hobbies _____

Sports _____ Food _____

Favorite things _____

Things (s)he can't stand_____

Does for fun _____

Bad habits _____

Fears _____

Quirks _____

Catchphrase _____

# Lesson 148: Antagonist Sidekick

Fill out this form for your antagonist's sidekick. Some may not apply. You can draw a picture of your sidekick in the box.

Name _____ Age _____

Job _____ Hair _____

Clothes _____ Home _____

Family _____ Music _____

Hobbies _____

Sports _____ Food _____

Favorite things _____

Things (s)he can't stand_____

Does for fun _____

Bad habits _____

Fears _____

Quirks _____

Catchphrase _____

Every story needs a conflict to make it exciting. What is yours? What does the hero try to do that the villain tries to stop? What incident will happen in the beginning of the book to set up the conflict? Jot down ideas to help you when you start writing.

_____

_____

_____

_____

_____

_____

_____

_____

**Think About It:** Conflict is the driving force of your story. As you're thinking about what your conflict is going to be, be sure to also think about the twists and turns your plot is going to take as a result of the conflict.

# Lesson 150: Specific Verbs

Write a specific verb for each of these verb and adverbs. Choosing more exciting words will make your book more exciting.

walked quickly _____

laughed crazily _____

talked slowly _____

walked proudly _____

laughed quietly _____

talked quickly _____

walked unevenly _____

laughed squeakily_____

talked loudly _____

**Did you know?** A new word is added to the English language every 98 minutes. That equates to more than 14 words a day and more than 5,000 words a year!

# Lesson 151: Writing – Setting

What is the overall setting of your book going to be? Fill in this page about your setting. You can use the bottom to sketch a picture of it if you'd like.

Time: _____

Description:_____

_____

_____

_____

_____

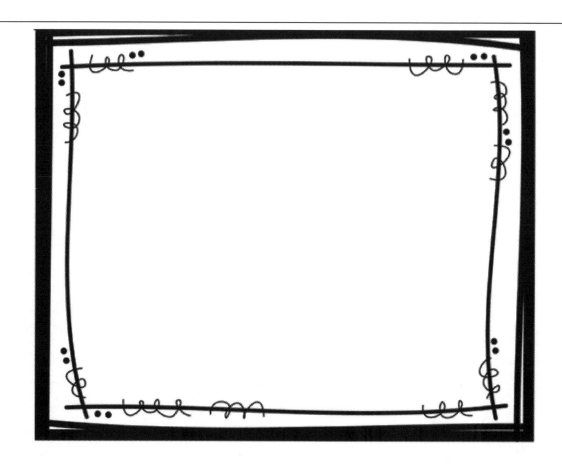

Today describe four different smaller settings in your book and what objects are in each one that might help or hinder your characters.

1. _____

Objects_____

_____

2. _____

Objects_____

_____

3. _____

Objects_____

_____

4. _____

Objects_____

_____

# Lesson 153: Writing

Do you know your basic story? Write out each of these steps for your book.

Background _____

_____

Incident that creates conflict _____

_____

Conflict _____

    Up _____

    Down_____

    Up _____

    Down _____

Climax _____

_____

Final Scene _____

_____

Let's think a little more about your story. There can be smaller stories within your story. Think about it. What would be the beginning, middle and end for your smaller story?

Beginning _____

_____

_____

_____

Middle _____

_____

_____

_____

End _____

_____

_____

_____

Fill out this chart for a book or movie you know really well.

Title:_____

| Main Character | Goal/Problem to Solve | Villain/Obstacle | Supporting Characters |
| --- | --- | --- | --- |
| | | | |

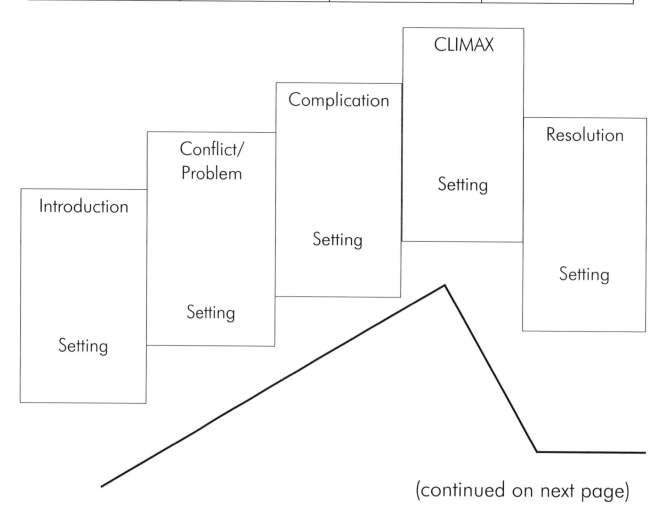

CLIMAX

Complication

Conflict/ Problem

Resolution

Setting

Introduction

Setting

Setting

Setting

Setting

Setting

(continued on next page)

# Lesson 155: Plot Chart

Now fill out this chart for your book.

Title:_____

| Main Character | Goal/Problem to Solve | Villain/Obstacle | Supporting Characters |
|---|---|---|---|
|  |  |  |  |

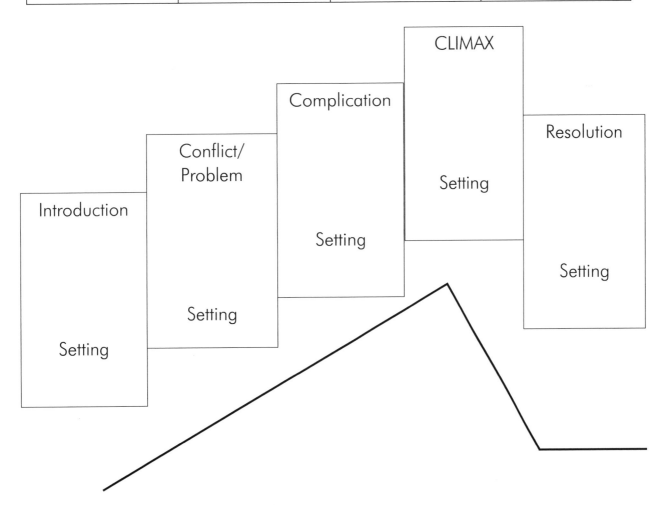

Fill out this chapter list with the plan for your chapters.

1)  Title/Situation: _____

    Setting: _____

2)  Title/Situation: _____

    Setting: _____

3)  Title/Situation: _____

    Setting: _____

4)  Title/Situation: _____

    Setting: _____

5)  Title/Situation: _____

    Setting: _____

6)  Title/Situation: _____

    Setting: _____

7)  Title/Situation: _____

    Setting: _____

8)  Title/Situation: _____

    Setting: _____

9)  Title/Situation: _____

    Setting: _____

10) Title/Situation: _____

    Setting: _____

# Congratulations!

You have finished Language Arts 5!

The Easy Peasy All-in-One Homeschool is a free, complete online homeschool curriculum. There are 180 days of ready-to-go assignments for every level and every subject. It's created for your children to work as independently as you want them to. Preschool through high school is available as well as courses ranging from English, math, science, and history to art, music, computer, thinking, physical education, and health. A daily Bible lesson is offered as well. The mission of Easy Peasy is to enable those to homeschool who otherwise thought they couldn't.

The Genesis Curriculum takes the Bible and turns it into lessons for your homeschool. Daily lessons include Bible reading, memory verse, spelling, handwriting, vocabulary, grammar, Biblical language, science, social studies, writing, and thinking through discussion questions.

The Genesis Curriculum uses a complete book of the Bible for one full year. The curriculum is being made using both Old and New Testament books. Find us online at genesiscurriculum.com to read about the latest developments in this expanding curriculum.

Made in United States
Orlando, FL
03 April 2024

45420316R00085